Offshore Sea Life ID Guide
West Coast

Steve N. G. Howell
Brian L. Sullivan

In collaboration with
Todd McGrath and
Tom Johnson

Princeton University Press Princeton and Oxford

Rowboat with a Blue Whale for scale!

Requests for permission to reproduce material from this work should be sent to
Permissions, Princeton University Press
Published by Princeton University Press, 41 William Street, Princeton, New Jersey 08540
In the United Kingdom: Princeton University Press, 6 Oxford Street, Woodstock, Oxfordshire OX20 1TW
press.princeton.edu

Cover image composite: Long-tailed Jaeger, Sabine's Gull, Tufted Puffin, Humpback Whale,
Pacific White-sided Dolphin, and Laysan Albatross © Brian L. Sullivan

Library of Congress Control Number: 2014951314
ISBN 978-0-691-16613-1 (pbk.)

British Library Cataloguing-in-Publication Data is available
This book has been composed in Minion Pro and Calibri
Printed on acid-free paper.
Printed in Malaysia
10 9 8 7 6 5 4 3 2 1

Offshore Sea Life ID Guide West Coast

Contents

A beautiful adult Steller's Albatross, like this, hasn't been seen off the West Coast for over 100 years—slaughter for the feather trade brought the species close to extinction. But with protection the population is increasing, and young birds are now visiting us from Japan (see pp. 46–47). Might you be the first to see an adult here?

Abbreviations. To save space we often use four-letter codes for species names; the codes are listed as an index on pp. 55–56. Likewise, standard state abbreviations are often used: CA California, OR Oregon, WA Washington, AK Alaska. For months we use 3 letters: Feb for February, Jun for June, etc. North, central, south, etc., are usually abbreviated as n., cen., s., etc. We use the Latin abbreviation cf. for 'compare with.'

Introduction

What do the following have in common? Majestic albatrosses sailing effortlessly over the ocean, huge whales sliding through the waves, silvery flyingfish shooting out from a ship's bow over glassy blue waters. Well, for the most part, you can't see them from shore. You'll need to experience these offshore wonders on a boat trip, often called a 'pelagic trip' by birdwatchers.

This identification guide uses composite plates of photos to help you identify offshore marine wildlife—'things you see at sea,' be they whales, birds, dolphins, sharks, sea lions, or jellyfish. Short accounts distill the essence of identification—wildlife views at sea can be brief, and the less time you spend reading a book the better. Once you have a name, numerous other resources are available to help you learn more about the creatures that inhabit the oceans. But that all-important handle, a species name, is the first step in the cascade of knowledge.

We focus on species seen on day trips off the West Coast (California, Oregon, Washington; see map inside back cover), not those found farther offshore in waters few people get to visit. Some of these species can be seen from shore but they also occur offshore and are usually considered marine creatures. We don't include coastal birds such as most gulls, terns, cormorants, sea ducks, loons, grebes, or even some 'marine' mammals (they're called *Harbor* Seals for a reason); even though you may see these from boats they can all be watched more easily from land. We also don't include real rarities, species you might never see even on 100 trips, such as a sea snake (below).

Yellow-bellied Sea Snake Pelamis platurus, *the most widespread reptile in the world, is seen only exceptionally off s. CA in warm water years. Adults reach 2–3 feet in length.*

On your way offshore you pass through the inshore zone (below), often alive with coastal 'seabirds,' such as gulls, pelicans, and cormorants, most of which tend to disappear when you get a mile or two offshore. Then you are in the world of shearwaters, dolphins, whales, and albatrosses—the pelagic zone.

Western Gulls

Elegant Tern

Heermann's Gull

Brown Pelican

Brandt's Cormorants

Brandt's Cormorant

Surf Scoter

Common Loon

Sea Otter

Harbor Seal

Out at sea, one thing you'll likely notice is that wildlife is not evenly distributed. Although the ocean all looks much the same from a boat, it comprises different habitats, much as land does—but on land we can easily see the difference between a field and a forest. Moreover, the habitats at sea are mobile, shifting with the currents and the wind. This means it can be difficult to predict where whales or birds will be from day to day, as they track their food resources across a seemingly featureless ocean.

Luckily, food tends to be concentrated in certain areas because of predictable marine processes. The food web starts with plankton, tiny organisms that fuel themselves with sunlight and nutrients, as plants do on land. Sunlight is easy to find anywhere near the surface (even on foggy days), but most of the nutrients in the ocean have sunk to the deep over countless ages. A process known as upwelling can bring nutrients up into reach of the sunlight, and thus set in motion the cycle of life.

Upwelling occurs in places where currents run into topographic features of the seabed, such as canyon walls or mountains (often known as 'banks' when they are high enough to approach the surface). The amazingly deep submarine canyon in Monterey Bay and the seamount known as Cordell Bank are two reasons the central California coast is such a hotspot for marine life.

Crab for dinner again? Sea Otters (like this mother and young) are an endearing feature of the Monterey area, but they are inshore creatures tied to the coastal kelp forests—so we don't consider them as offshore sea life.

Another important upwelling region, where underwater currents run into topography, is where the continental shelf drops off to the deep. The shelf is the relatively shallow seabed that extends from a continental landmass. The point at which it ends and the seabed drops off steeply is known as the 'shelf break.' Along most of the West Coast the continental shelf is relatively narrow, and the shelf break can be reached easily in a day trip. Marine life is usually much more abundant in this region than in either the shelf waters inshore of the break or the deeper waters well offshore.

Dense swarming masses of Sooty Shearwaters gather locally off the West Coast in summer to molt, and at times can be seen from shore. However, these seemingly huge numbers (which in part inspired The Birds, *Alfred Hitchcock's classic horror movie), are a fraction of those seen here in the 1980s. Reasons for this decline remain unclear.*

While offshore wildlife includes spectacular animals such as whales and albatrosses, as well as some birds in great abundance, the total number of species is manageable. In the region this guide covers, we consider only about 20 mammals and 40 bird species as regularly occurring offshore marine creatures. To balance this modest number, however, many of the species look quite similar, and viewing wildlife from a moving platform can be a challenge.

Medications can help with seasickness (if taken ahead of time), but many people do just fine on boats if they stay outside with the breeze in their face and a view of the horizon (don't sit in the cabin and read!). The ocean has a finite range of motions, and observing swell direction and moving your body accordingly is a good idea—learn to move with the ocean, not fight against it. Off the West Coast on a boat it can be colder than you think, even (or especially!) in summer, when it may be sunny and even hot onshore. It's better to bring extra clothes and not need them than to spend the day cold and uncomfortable.

Often the best and easiest viewing is when the boat is stopped, either because whales have been spotted or because birds are coming in to feed on 'chum' (food put out for them). Most wildlife can be appreciated simply with the naked eye, but binoculars are helpful when looking for smaller birds such as storm-petrels and phalaropes.

Now all that remains is to get out there and experience the magic of the open ocean. Enjoy!

Killer Whale putting on a show!

Bow-riding Northern Right-whale and Pacific White-sided Dolphins.

A 'friendly' Humpback Whale brushing against the boat!

Acknowledgments

During more than 50 years of combined experience going out on boats to look for birds, mammals, and other marine creatures we have met many who share our passion, far too many to name here. In connection with our West Coast trips we particularly thank Terry Hunefeld, Todd McGrath, Ken Petersen, Peter Pyle, and Debi Shearwater. Others who helped in different ways include Elaine Cook, Megan Elrod, Burr Heneman, Diana Humple, Dennis Jongsomjit, Jackie Sones, and Rollo Turner. Most photos used here are our own, but we thank collaborators Todd McGrath and Tom Johnson, along with Jennifer Green, Beth Hamel, Ryan Merrill, Ben Saenz, and Melanie White/Granite State Whale Watch for sharing their images.

Books offering additional information about West Coast sea life include *Field Guide to Marine Mammals of the Pacific Coast* by S. G. Allen et al. (2011), *Whales, Dolphins, and Other Marine Mammals of the World* by H. Shirihai and B. Jarrett (2006), the pioneering *Ocean Birds of the Nearshore Pacific* by R. Stallcup (1990), and *Petrels, Albatrosses, and Storm-Petrels of North America* by S. N. G. Howell (2012).

Some Words Explained

Alcid (pronounced 'al-sid'): Any member of the auk family, including murres, puffins, guillemots, auklets, and murrelets.

Blow: The spray blown skyward by a breathing whale.

Breaching: To leap clear or almost clear of the water.

Fluking: Raising of tail flukes above the sea surface as a marine mammal dives.

Footprint: Slick area of water displaced at the surface as a whale sounds.

Jug-handling: To lie at the sea surface with flippers linked, looking like a jug handle (see p. 23).

Logging: To lie at the sea surface, looking like a floating log.

Pelagic: Relating to the open ocean.

Porpoising: A mode of fast travel (used mainly by dolphins and sea lions) involving repeated low-angle leaps from the water (the air offers less resistance than water).

Sounding: The action of a marine mammal diving to stay down for a while and leaving a 'footprint' at the surface.

Spy-hopping: To raise the head straight up out of the water, apparently to look around above the surface.

Tubenose: Any bird in the order Procellariiformes, which have nostrils housed in tubes on the bill, including albatrosses, shearwaters, petrels, and storm-petrels.

Marine Mammals

Unlike seabirds, marine mammals spend most of their time underwater, coming to the surface to breathe, and rarely do you see the whole animal. Views can be brief, and we provide the clues needed to identify species based on what you are likely to see—a fin, a blow, a head looking around.

As with 'seabirds,' some 'marine' mammals live along the coast, such as Harbor Seals and Sea Otters. We do not treat these species because they are not really offshore creatures; they can be seen more easily from land. Other marine mammals can be seen from shore on occasion, such as Gray Whales on their annual migrations, although to see them up close you'll still want to go out on a boat.

Things to look for when identifying whales and dolphins are group size, general behavior, dorsal fin size and shape, any patterns or markings, and, for the larger whales, shape and size of the blow and how soon the dorsal fin appears relative to when you see the blow. For sea lions and fur seals (collectively known as pinnipeds) note behavior, head shape (especially in profile), overall coloration, and prominence of ears and whiskers.

adult male and young Killer Whale

spy-hopping

adult female

*adult male fin tall
but quite variable*

Killer Whale (Orca) (KIWH)

Striking and sought-after, this large dolphin (not a true whale) can be found year-round, most reliably in 'inland' waters of WA (Puget Sound and San Juan Islands). Uncommon offshore, mainly spring and fall. Unmistakable if seen well, but at a distance cf. Risso's Dolphin (p. 18). Blow puffy, usually not conspicuous. Often first detected when fin of adult male towers out of the water. Females and younger males have smaller fins. Seen singly or in small groups, often moving quickly; can be difficult to keep track of. On occasion can be seen hunting seals or whales, putting on a spectacular if bloody show.

splash after breach

blow variable

pectoral flippers waving

fluke pattern highly variable

lumpy, variable dorsal fin

blowholes

Humpback Whale (HUWH)

The staple of many whale-watching businesses. Occurs mainly Apr–Oct, especially fall, but can be seen in any month. Well known for active displays at the surface, including tail-slapping, breaching (see front cover), and lunge feeding. Often seen simply blowing, swimming, and diving (arching its back high but not fluking). With luck, can be seen fluking before deeper dives. Blow bushy but fairly high, can be mistaken for Blue Whale blow on calm days. Dorsal fin distinctive but variable, lumpy and fairly low; very long narrow flippers mostly white. Underside of flukes variable; many individuals can be identified by tail pattern.

distant blow

blow before surfacing

small, variable dorsal fin

blowholes

Blue Whale (BLWH)

Largest mammal known to have existed on our planet. Fairly common locally off CA, mainly summer–fall, rare elsewhere. Singly or in small groups, at times of 20+ animals associating with other whales at rich feeding areas, especially with HUWH off cen. CA, with FIWH off s. CA. At times quite close to shore. Blow very tall and straight (or bushy but strong before breaking surface). Massive and broad-bodied but has surprisingly small, nub-like dorsal fin (individually variable) that appears well after the blow and after a long stretch of broad, smooth back slides by. Pale gray ('blue') coloration often striking. Flukes fairly often, but rarely breaches.

Gray Whale (GRWH)

Common migrant, heading s. to Mexico in Oct–Dec, n. to Alaska in Mar–May; small numbers occur at other seasons, mainly summer–fall; a few give birth off s. CA, as around the Channel Islands. Often close to shore and regularly seen from land, at times in loose groups. Puffy blow often inconspicuous. Gray overall, usually with variable pale markings; head often encrusted with whitish barnacles. Lacks dorsal fin, but 'knuckled' tail stock distinctive. Sometimes breaches, and shows flukes when diving deeper; more often simply swims fairly low in the water and rolls gently before diving.

Fin Whale (FIWH)

Fairly common off s. CA (mainly summer–fall, but present year-round), rarely seen northward, usually well offshore; singly or in small groups. Very large and often fast swimming, with sloping dorsal fin typically wider at base than tall, slightly falcate (individually quite variable; cf. much smaller MIWH). Tall straight blow averages lower than BLWH blow. Fin appears after blow and after a stretch of back rolls by. Dark slaty gray above; often looks blackish, but can appear paler when reflecting bright light. Sides of lower jaw differ in color: left side blackish, right side white. Rarely flukes or breaches.

right side of lower jaw white on Fin Whale

Northern Minke Whale (MIWH)

The Minke (pronounced 'minky') is perhaps fairly common off the West Coast, but is inconspicuous and thus seen infrequently. Present year-round, inshore to offshore, usually singly. Fairly small and fast swimming; resembles a mini FIWH, but dorsal fin typically taller than wide, often more falcate. Blow low and bushy, usually not striking; fin appears simultaneously with blow, not after a length of back has appeared (as in FIWH). Short flippers have contrasting whitish band (difficult to see). Often rolls fairly high but rarely flukes, and after a few blows tends to disappear. Infrequent breaches can be clear out of the water.

lacks dorsal fin

'knuckled' tail stock

sloping fin wide at base, appears well after blow

long back

falcate, shark-like fin appears with blow

blowholes

Risso's Dolphin (RIDO)

Uncommon to fairly common off CA, this large dolphin is usually seen in small to moderately large groups, occasionally mixing with other species; infrequently seen off OR and WA. Rarely bow-rides, and often indifferent to boats; can move fast and sometimes breaches. Does not usually porpoise clear of the water. Note prominent, tall dorsal fin, blunt head, fairly large size. Dorsal fin shape highly variable (cf. female Killer Whale, p. 13; Bottlenose Dolphin). Coloration also variable, from milky whitish to dark gray; adults often extensively scratched.

Common Bottlenose Dolphin (BODO)

Stereotypical, playful dolphin of aquariums and feel-good movies. Uncommon to fairly common in warmer inshore waters of s. CA, n. locally to cen. CA. Often seen from shore cruising just beyond the breakers, where it can be mistaken for a large shark but usually in small groups. Offshore populations, living beyond the continental shelf, also occur off s. CA. Fairly large with prominent, falcate dorsal fin (cf. Risso's Dolphin), stubby beak (often with white-tipped lower jaw), and rather plain, dark gray coloration. At times acrobatic, leaping high and tail-slapping, and often bow-rides; at other times simply swims by, indifferent to boats.

Common Dolphins (CODO)

Common off s. CA, ranging n. in small numbers to cen. CA (mainly fall–winter in warmer water years). Off s. CA, often in large, fast-moving, and acrobatic groups (at times in 1000s), splashing the surface into a white frenzy. Handsome side pattern easily seen as animals leap and bow-ride. Dorsal fin smaller, darker, and less falcate than Pacific White-sided Dolphin (p. 21). Scientists have recognized 2 species of 'Common Dolphin' since the mid-1990s: Short-beaked and Long-beaked, which can be difficult to distinguish at sea, although they rarely if ever mix. Long-beaked occurs in warmer, shallower waters over the shelf, Short-beaked occurs in deeper offshore waters.

Within a school of Common Dolphins it is usually possible to see (or photograph) at least a few animals showing features that support species identification. Both species variable, but Short-beaked has a shorter beak (overlaps with some Long-beaked), steeper forehead, 'cuter' facial expression, and more strongly contrasting creamy side patches that lack a narrow dark line along the lower edge, as shown by many Long-beaked. When in doubt, best to identify simply as 'Common Dolphin sp.' (sp. = species unknown).

large, with blunt head, tall fin

short 'bottlenose' beak

Short-beaked Common Dolphins

Short-beaked Common

Long-beaked Common

'cuter' face
brighter pattern

dark sideline

Northern Right-whale Dolphin (NRDO)

Fairly common and distinctive. Mainly in cooler waters off cen. CA (s. to n. Channel Islands), ranging to s. CA in winter, n. to OR and WA mainly in summer. Looks like a sleek black sausage; most often confused with porpoising sea lions. Usually in small to fairly large groups (at times 100s), mixing readily with Pacific White-sided Dolphins; the 2 species often bow-ride together. White 'tuxedo' belly pattern rarely seen unless animal breaches; occasional individuals have white extending up to lower sides of body and are more obviously bicolored.

Pacific White-sided Dolphin (PWDO)

Common and distinctive; favors cooler waters, often at the shelf-break or where different water masses meet. Usually in groups, from 5–20 individuals to 100s. Mixes readily with Northern Right-whale Dolphins, and the 2 species often bow-ride together. Note falcate, two-tone dorsal fin, short blunt beak; striking 'white-sided' pattern best seen when animals jump. Acrobatic and often leaps from water, at times spinning and flipping head over tail; at other times elusive and indifferent to boats.

Dall's Porpoise (DAPO)

Fairly common, mainly in cooler shelf and offshore waters. Often detected by distinctive 'rooster tail' of spray as dorsal fin slashes surface. Small, stocky, and fast, usually in small groups, not mixing with other species. Often bow-rides but does not leap (frustratingly difficult to photograph); sometimes rolls slowly at the surface. Striking black-and-white pattern distinctive but variable. In Pacific Northwest, rare hybrids with Harbor Porpoise show intermediate features.

Harbor Porpoise (HAPO)

Fairly common but inconspicuous small porpoise of cooler inshore waters and tidal rips from cen. CA northward, at times s. to Point Conception. Found singly or in small groups. Often seen from shore, rolling just beyond the breakers; unlikely to be seen far offshore. 'Hershey's Kiss' dorsal fin lacks white tip of Dall's Porpoise fin. Usually surfaces 2-3 times before disappearing, but at times can swim quickly and create splashes. Usually indifferent to boats and rarely bow-rides.

'tuxedo' pattern

lacks dorsal fin

falcate, bicolored fin

'rooster tail' splashes

inconspicuous, with low triangular dorsal fin

California Sea Lion (CASL)

Noisy and familiar along and off coast of CA, ranges n. to WA (mainly fall–winter). Occasionally in large groups, especially in fall. Note dog-like head shape with pointed snout; adult male has distinct forehead bump. Sometimes 'jug-handles' like NOFS, but flippers and whiskers shorter; note nose shape. Fast-moving animals leap in porpoising mode like dolphins.

traveling sea lions

Steller's (Northern) Sea Lion (STSL)

Fairly common off WA, becoming uncommon off cen. CA, rare off s. CA. Large and heavyset, more massive than CASL, with bigger, bear-like head and blunter nose; adults paler, more golden in color than most CASL. Low growling calls distinct from dog-like barks of CASL. Aggressive; often scavenges at fishing boats. Population declining for reasons that remain poorly understood.

Northern Fur Seal (NOFS)

Uncommon, but seen regularly throughout the region, especially in fall–winter. Usually singles or 2s and 3s well offshore. Note very long whiskers and flippers, distinctive snub-nosed profile, more 'innocent' expression than CASL. Often rests in 'jug-handling' position. Breeds mainly on islands in the Bering Sea, but with 2 smaller West Coast colonies on California's Farallon and Channel Islands.

Guadalupe Fur Seal (GUFS)

Uncommon visitor off s. CA, mainly in spring–fall from breeding grounds on Guadalupe Island, Mexico; very rarely n. in fall to n. CA. Looks more like CASL than NOFS, but has narrower, more pointed snout than CASL and more prominent, 'elf-like' ears. Considered extinct in 1900 (hunted for the fur trade) but rediscovered in 1950s at Guadalupe; increasing with protection, and has bred in recent years on California Channel Islands.

Northern Elephant Seal (NESE)

Best known on land, where breeding groups gather locally at beaches in Dec–Mar. Occurs year-round throughout region, but found infrequently at sea, usually single animals well offshore. At a distance looks like a deadhead log riding high in the water; usually sinks before close approach.

females/immatures

forehead bump

adult male

*broad, bear-like head
paler color than CASL*

females/immatures

'jug-handling'

snub-nosed profile

'jug-handling'

pointed nose

immatures

immatures

'deadhead
log'

Sperm Whale (SPWH)

Seen occasionally, mainly spring and fall in deep water well offshore; singly (mainly males) or in loose groups (mainly females and young). Bushy blow angled forward, not vertical. Dorsal fin low and bluntly triangular; massive head apparent at closer range; rear of body wrinkled. Rests at the surface (looks like a giant turd), blowing frequently before sounding for a deep dive, when usually shows its broad, triangular flukes. Feeds on squid in deep water, and dives can be as long as 1–2 hours!

Short-finned Pilot Whale (SFPW)

Found in deep water off s. CA, exceptional elsewhere. Obviously larger than typical dolphins, smaller than true whales. Usually in groups of 10–50, often logging at the surface; rarely breaches or shows flukes. Blackish overall, with blunt head; dorsal fin low and wide-based, lobed at tip on adult male. Occasionally curious around boats, but often indifferent and can swim away fairly quickly. Feeding dives usually 10–20 minutes. 'Short' refers to the pectoral flippers (rarely visible), not the dorsal fin.

Baird's Beaked Whale (BABW)

Rarely seen, but most frequently encountered beaked whale on day trips off West Coast. Obviously larger than dolphins, smaller than typical whales. Usually in fairly tight groups of 3–30. Low bushy blows fairly synchronous as animals log at the surface before deep dives; usually down at least 10–30 minutes. At times flukes and breaches. Long-bodied, with long blunt beak; overall dark brown or gray, often marked with scratches. Dorsal fin variable, typically triangular.

Cuvier's Beaked Whale (CUBW)

Can be found off s. CA, mainly in deep water around Channel Islands and sea mounts; rare elsewhere in deep water offshore. Larger than dolphins, clearly smaller than typical whales. Singly or in groups of 2–5. Low bushy blow inconspicuous. Color varies from dark to pale; adults have whitish head, and adult male is marked with whitish scratches. Surfacing animals often show distinctive short 'goosebeak.' Rolls fairly high before diving, but does not fluke; rarely breaches. Dives usually 20–40 minutes, but can descend to almost 2 miles deep and stay down 2 hours!

blow angled forward

broad triangular flukes

wide-based dorsal fin

synchronous bushy blows

long blunt beak

slightly falcate fin

adult male has tooth at tip of beak

'goosebeak' face profile

Seabirds

True seabirds live mainly beyond sight of shore, and include the tube-noses such as albatrosses, shearwaters, and storm-petrels, and the alcids (diving birds including puffins, murres, and auklets). Many tubenoses are long-distance migrants that breed in the Southern Hemisphere, whereas West Coast alcids are shorter-distance migrants that breed in the North Pacific.

Black-footed Albatrosses often swim right up to the back of boats, allowing their subtle beauty to be appreciated.

with adult Western Gull

immature

immature

adult

adult

Black-footed Albatross (BFAL)

Common offshore spring–fall, uncommon in winter. Often follows boats and scavenges. Dark overall with white 'noseband,' dusky bill. Older adult has white tail coverts; some birds bleach to whitish on head and neck. Breeds Nov–Jun mainly in Hawaii.

Laysan Albatross (LAAL)

Uncommon offshore year-round; commoner off s. CA in spring, off n. CA to WA in fall–winter. Suggests a large, dark-backed gull but has dark tail, variable black underwing pattern. Immature has white face, adult has grayish cheeks. Breeds Nov–Jun in Hawaii and nw. Mexico.

contrasting white flash

small bill

Sooty Shearwater (SOSH)

Commonest dark-bodied shearwater off West Coast, locally in 1000s; can be seen from shore (see p. 8). Mainly Apr–Oct; a few in winter. Note silvery-white flash under wings. Breeds Nov–Apr in Chile and New Zealand.

Short-tailed Shearwater (STSH)

Uncommon, mainly late fall–winter. Very similar to Sooty Shearwater but has smaller bill. Duller underwings lack strong contrast between whitish coverts and dark primaries; flight quicker, snappier. Breeds Nov–Apr in Australia.

stocky overall
stout pale bill

plumage highly
variable (see p. 31)
typically grayer
than shearwaters

Flesh-footed Shearwater (FFSH)

Uncommon, mainly fall. Like PFSH (p. 30) in size, shape, and flight manner but all-dark; note pink bill with black tip. Usually in 1s and 2s, often in rafts with other shearwaters. Breeds Nov–Apr in New Zealand.

Northern Fulmar (NOFU)

Mainly late fall–winter. Numbers vary year to year, often scarce s. of cen. CA. Will scavenge boldly, locally in 100s. Stockier than shearwaters, with bulbous head, stout pale bill. Plumage variable some have white head and body (p. 31).

underparts with variable dark markings

underparts clean white

Pink-footed Shearwater (PFSH)
Common spring–fall, small numbers in winter. Largest shearwater, with broader wings, more relaxed flight than SOSH. Note dark head sides, smudgy underwings; pink bill with black tip easier to see than pink feet. Breeds Nov–Apr in Chile.

Buller's Shearwater (BUSH)
Uncommon to fairly common in mid–late fall, very rare in spring–summer. Handsome, with patterned upperparts, clean dark cap. Flight usually buoyant and graceful, low to the water. Breeds Nov–Apr in New Zealand.

small shearwater, flight low and hurried

plumage highly variable (see p. 29)

Northern Fulmar (NOFU)

See p. 29 for dark morph, commoner off West Coast than light morph. Plumage highly variable. Can suggest a gull but rump and tail pale gray, flies with wings held stiffly, bill stout and tube-nosed. Breeds May–Sep in Alaska.

Black-vented Shearwater (BVSH)

Common off s. CA, mainly fall–winter, irregular n. to n. CA. Often seen from shore, at times in 1000s. Like mini PFSH but has slender dark bill; hurried flight usually low to the water. Breeds Mar–Aug in Baja California, Mexico.

Storm-Petrels. Very small seabirds, resembling bats or swallows, that fly low over the water; often difficult to see well and identify to species. Usually encountered singly or in loose flocks, but in fall can be seen locally in rafts of 1000s, mainly from San Diego n. to Cordell Bank. Most species have forked tails, not just Fork-tailed Storm-Petrel. White-rumped species are on p. 34.

smoky gray plumage can look silvery in bright sunlight

plumage ashier, less blackish than BLSP

pale underwing stripe

Fork-tailed Storm-Petrel (FTSP)

Common offshore in North Pacific, ranging s. to cen. CA (mainly fall–winter), rarely to s. CA. Note contrasting black underwing coverts. Flight low and fluttery in calm, but banks and wheels in strong winds.

Ashy Storm-Petrel (ASSP)

Fairly common off CA year-round; fall concentrations of 1000s off cen. coast. Flight fairly direct and fluttery with short glides. Fall birds often molting, can look short-tailed. Off s. CA cf. Chapman's Storm-Petrel (see Leach's Storm-Petrel, p. 34).

Black

Ashy

Least

Fork-tailed

tapered tail

Black Storm-Petrel (BLSP)
Common off s. CA May–Oct; in fall ranges n. to cen. CA. Largest storm-petrel in the region, twice the size of ASSP. Flies with languid deep wingbeats, frequent glides. Often follows boats off s. CA; occurs in rafts with ASSP off cen. CA.

Least Storm-Petrel (LTSP)
Fall visitor off San Diego from Mexico, in some years a few reach cen. CA. Often in rafts of BLSP off s. CA. Smaller and blacker than ASSP, suggests mini BLSP. Flight quick and erratic with deep jerky wingbeats and no gliding.

Leach's Storm-Petrel complex (left side of page) includes widespread, white-rumped birds known as Leach's; dark-rumped birds off s. CA known as Chapman's Storm-Petrel; and little-known Townsend's Storm-Petrel (TOSP), a late summer–fall visitor from Mexico to s. CA. Townsend's can be white-rumped or dark-rumped, often not safely told from Leach's and Chapman's.

Chapman's

Townsend's/ Chapman's

Townsend's

long legs

forked tail

Leach's

toes project

Leach's Storm-Petrel (LHSP)

Fairly common spring–fall, mainly well offshore. Typical flight strong and bounding, with wings held crooked. Townsend's averages shorter tail, larger white rump. Chapman's lacks pale underwing stripe of Ashy Storm-Petrel (p. 32).

Wilson's Storm-Petrel (WISP)

Scarce spring–fall visitor from Antarctica, mainly Aug–Oct. Wings shorter and straighter than Leach's, more swallow-like; flight usually direct and fluttery; at times patters on surface. Feet project beyond tail tip (difficult to see).

Phalaropes are small sandpipers that swim. They breed on Arctic tundra and winter at sea; often in flocks, sometimes of 1000s.

breeding plumage

immature/non-breeding plumage

molting adults

Red Phalarope (REPH)

Common migrant offshore (mainly May, Jul–Nov); some winter off CA. Larger and bulkier than Red-necked Phalarope, with thicker bill, bolder white wingstripe. Fall migrants look relatively large and silvery, can be mistaken for FTSP (p. 32).

Red-necked Phalarope (RNPH)

Common migrant inshore to off-shore (mainly Apr–May, Jul–Oct), often along current edges, on glassy strips of water; mixes readily with Red Phalarope. Note very fine, all-black bill; in fall, often looks black-and-white overall. Winters s. of US.

Small Alcids. Unless seas are calm it can be very difficult to spot small alcids on the water. They are shy of moving boats and usually seen flying away. Auklets run on the water before take-off, murrelets can spring into the air. Xantus's Murrelet (shown in many field guides) was split in 2012 into 2 species: Guadalupe and Scripps's Murrelets (opposite page).

often struggles to take off

immature has dusky eyes

bold white neck sides
gray back

adult

non-breeding/immature

Cassin's Auklet (CAAU)

Common locally; found in 1000s on some trips, missed on others. Often too full of food to fly from approaching boats. Grapefruit-size, with rounded head. Slaty gray overall, with white belly; white eyebrows visible at close range.

Ancient Murrelet (ANMU)

Uncommon to fairly common offshore, mainly Oct–Mar, commoner northward. Singly or in groups. Boldly patterned, with short pale bill. Breeding plumage has black throat, grizzled ('ancient') white streaks behind eye.

Guadalupe Murrelet (GUMU)

Non-breeding visitor Jul–Oct from Mexico; best known off s. and cen. CA, but also occurs n. to WA, usually well offshore. Like SCMU but dark eye stands out in white face.

Scripps's

often in pairs

all ages of both species similar

non-breeding/immature

Scripps's   Guadalupe

white face

breeding plumage

Scripps's

Marbled Murrelet (MAMU)

Uncommon to fairly common, in 1s and 2s; rarely found more than a mile or two offshore. Breeding plumage mottled brown. Non-breeding and immature boldly patterned; note white back patches. Cf. Common Murre chick (p. 38).

Scripps's Murrelet (SCMU)

Locally common off s. CA Apr–Jun, ranging n. offshore to OR and WA in Jul–Oct. Found in 1s and 2s. Note dark face, often with white notch forward of eye; underwings bright white overall (cf. Craveri's Murrelet, pp. 46–47).

breeding plumage adult with chick

messy dark-and-white pattern

dagger-like bill, clean dark-and-white pattern

non-breeding/ immature

non-breeding plumage

breeding plumage

Common Murre (COMU)

Common WA to cen. CA, uncommon s. CA. Inshore to offshore, often in 10s or 100s, loosely mixed with cormorants, gulls, etc. In summer–fall, adult male travels with chick (male has gutteral growls, chick has reedy whistles).

Pigeon Guillemot (PIGU)

Common breeder s. to n. Channel Islands; in Sep–Feb most move n. to inshore waters of WA to AK. Mainly inshore, often seen from land. Non-breeding plumages told from Common Murre by messier plumage, white wing panel, shorter bill.

whitish belly *(dark on puffin)*

immatures *(note head and bill shapes)*

breeding plumage

'Rhino' Puffin

breeding plumage

non-breeding plumage

non-breeding plumage

Rhinoceros Auklet (RHAU)

Common WA and OR, breeding locally s. to CA, where commoner in winter. Singly or in groups; can mix with murres. Football-size, with anvil-shaped head, orange bill. Adult loses bill horn in fall; immature bill dull and slender.

Tufted Puffin (TUPU)

Locally common breeder Apr–Aug WA and OR, in small numbers s. to cen. CA; winters in deep offshore waters. Usually singly at sea. Immature has deeper bill, more rounded head than Rhinoceros Auklet.

Tropicbird and Booby

red bill
black mask

immature has
brown belly

long tail

adult female

adult male has
whitish crown

Red-billed Tropicbird (RBTR)

Scarce in summer–fall off s. CA, usually well offshore. Singly or in 2s, separate from other seabirds. Often appears 'magically' overhead, at other times seen as a distant white speck on the water. Wingbeats hurried, ungraceful, unlike large terns.

Brown Booby (BRBO)

Scarce but increasing off CA (mainly summer–fall), exceptionally to WA. Large, streamlined diving seabird, found singly. Flight strong and direct, low to high. Associates with gulls and pelicans; roosts on inshore rocks, harbor markers, jetties.

wing molt

chasing California Gull

South Polar Skua (SPSK)

Uncommon migrant from Antarctic regions, mainly Aug–Oct; also in spring off s. CA. Like a large, powerful, dark gull with white wing flashes; many birds here are in wing molt. Strong direct flight low to high over the water. Chases larger gulls, shearwaters, etc., to steal food. Usually singly or in 2s and 3s, often around flocks of shearwaters. Cf. dark Pomarine Jaeger (p. 42), which has more slender bill, usually some pale barring on tail coverts.

Jaegers (pronounced 'yay-gers'). Resemble dark, streamlined gulls; all 3 species have whitish wing flashes. Plumage highly variable, especially immatures; often difficult to identify to species. Pomarine and Parasitic adults have a dark morph. Breed on Arctic tundra and spend non-breeding periods at sea. Feed by pirating other seabirds, forcing them to regurgitate their food.

breeding plumage adults

dark morph

'spoon-tipped'

subadult

winter adult

immatures

subadults

Pomarine Jaeger (POJA)

Largest jaeger, fairly common spring and fall, scarce in winter. All ages have thick, blunt-tipped tail projections (long and 'spoon-tipped' on adults); also note relatively big bill, broad wings. As on other jaegers, underwing coverts barred on immature, solidly dark on adult. Often in wing molt in fall. Sometimes follows boats, associates on water with shearwater flocks; chases larger gulls and shearwaters.

breeding plumage adults

sharp point

often broken or shed in fall

subadult

dark morph

strong contrast

immatures

crescent of white shafts

2 white shafts

Parasitic Jaeger (PAJA)

Medium-size, fairly common spring and fall, scarce in winter n. to cen. CA, nearer shore than other jaegers. Angular and falcon-like, with pointed tail projections. Immature often warm-toned (some all-dark). Chases terns and gulls.

Long-tailed Jaeger (LTJA)

Smallest jaeger, fairly common fall migrant, rare in spring; winters s. of US. Graceful, with long slender tail, 2–3 white shafts on upperwing. Immature cold-toned (some all-dark). Chases terns, smaller gulls, storm-petrels.

Gulls and Terns

immatures

breeding plumage adults

non-breeding plumages

bold wing pattern distinctive

solid black wing-tip

Black-legged Kittiwake (BLKI)

Fairly common offshore, Oct–Apr; numbers vary between years, sometimes stays into summer. Fairly small, long-winged gull. Adult has solid black wing-tip, plain yellow bill; immature has black M-pattern across upperwings. Breeds in North Pacific.

Sabine's Gull (SAGU)

Uncommon to fairly common migrant, Jul–Oct, usually well offshore; rarely late spring. Small, elegant gull with bright white triangles on upperwing, tern-like flight. Singly or in flocks of 10s. Breeds on Arctic tundra, winters mainly off South America.

narrower
black

contrast

translucent

immatures

distinct
blackish

whitish
(dark on
Common)

uniform
no contrast

contrast

longer bill
black tip

breeding plumage adults

Arctic Tern (ARTE)

Fairly common migrant offshore, May and Aug–Sep. Medium-small tern with long narrow wings; mostly translucent primaries lack contrast of adult COTE. Many birds not easily identified given typical views, best called Common/Arctic. Winters in Antarctica.

Common Tern (COTE)

Fairly common migrant inshore to offshore, Apr–May and Jul–Oct. Longer head/neck/bill than ARTE, smoother wingbeats. Lacks translucent wings of ARTE and has thicker black trailing edge to outer wing; immature has blacker leading edge to inner wing. Winters s. of US.

Craveri's Murrelet (CRMU)

This small alcid is an irregular late summer–fall visitor (absent some years) from Mexico to s. CA; in El Niño years can reach cen. CA. Much like Scripps's Murrelet (p. 37) but sleeker, with finer bill, longer tail often cocked in point; also note deeper black cap with no white notch forward of eye. Underwings variably dusky overall, not gleaming white like Scripps's.

Manx Shearwater (MASH)

Rare but increasing, mainly inshore in fall–spring. Small black-and-white shearwater with clean white undertail coverts. Flight snappier than Black-vented Shearwater (p. 31); towers steeply into and across strong winds. Breeds Apr–Sep in North Atlantic, recent colonist in North Pacific.

Black-vented

Manx

white

Steller's (Short-tailed) Albatross (STAL)

Thought extinct in 1930s, but has recovered with protection and now over 2500 birds range over the cold North Pacific (breeds late Oct–Jun in Japan). A few occur each year off West Coast, mainly Aug–Apr but has been seen in all months. Usually in association with smaller Black-footed and Laysan Albatrosses. All ages easily identified by huge, pale pink bill. All recent records are of dark brown immatures (cf. Black-footed) but some subadults have reached British Columbia. See adult photo on p. 4.

Steller's (left) with Black-footed Albatross, Northern Fulmars, and immature gulls.

*dusky underwing coverts
(cf. SCMU on p. 37)*

subadults

immatures

Gadfly Petrels. Petrels in the genus *Pterodroma* are known as gadfly petrels, for their impetuous, high arcing flight. Many birders consider them as the ultimate seabirds, and any day you see a gadfly petrel is special. They tend to stay well offshore, over deep waters beyond the continental shelf. On occasion, however, they stray nearer shore, and these 3 species are sometimes seen on day trips off the West Coast.

Cook's Petrel (COPE). Fairly common far off West Coast, especially s. and cen. California in Apr–Sep; in some years ranges nearer shore. Usually seen singly, but can be found in loose flocks. Small, fast-flying petrel with bright white underparts. Gray upperparts have dark M pattern and can blend easily against gray waters. Breeds Nov–Mar in New Zealand.

Cook's Petrels

Hawaiian Petrel (HAPE). Scarce, but increasingly found off West Coast, mainly Apr–Sep off California. Usually seen singly. Medium-size petrel, dark above with blackish cap, white forehead blaze; white below with bold black underwing margins. Breeds Apr–Oct in Hawaii. Formerly known as Dark-rumped Petrel.

Murphy's Petrel (MUPE). Fairly common some years far off West Coast, mainly Mar–May. Singly or in loose groups. Medium-size, dark-bodied petrel. Slightly smaller than Sooty Shearwater (p. 28), with longer tail, shorter thicker bill, and more dynamic, buoyant flight with wings held crooked. Note gray gloss to upperparts, silvery underwing flashes on primaries, whitish at base of bill. Breeds Jun–Dec in tropical Pacific.

Other Sea Life

Ocean Sunfish (Mola) *Mola mola*. The seas are home to many fish, but most are not easily viewed from a boat. An exception is the bizarre Mola, which can be seen floating at the surface, singly or in loose groups. Laterally compressed, it often lies on its side, looking like a trashcan lid and loosely waving a shark-like fin above the surface. The largest Molas can be over 10 feet across and weigh over 2 tons.

Mola fin

Mola hunting Velella (see p. 53)

Sharks are seen occasionally on pelagic trips, most often the slender and sleek Blue Shark *Prionace glauca* (usually 3–8 feet long off CA). Most shark species are not readily identified in the field, and usually all you get is a brief view of a dorsal fin and sometimes the tail fin—a bit of an anticlimax if you are hoping for a *Jaws*-type encounter. Beware: the fins of Molas and the flippers of sea lions can be mistaken for sharks.

Unidentified shark species, a typical view

Flyingfish. Of 60 or so species worldwide, a few occur off s. CA (mainly in summer–fall), but are not readily identified to species; the commonest species here is *Cheilopogon pinnatibarbatus*, one of the largest of all flyingfish. Usually 6–18 inches long with 'wingspans' up to 2 feet or so, flyingfish shoot out of the water and glide away from approaching boats, as if escaping from a predator (which is why they fly). The tail acts like a propeller and can kick a zig-zag wake in the water surface to power extra flights, at times for hundreds of yards.

Unidentified flyingfish (possibly *Cheilopogon pinnatibarbatus*)

Blue Sharks

Mola and immature California Gull

Sea Turtles are mainly animals of warmer waters; it's a special day if you see one off the West Coast. The least infrequently seen is **Leatherback Turtle** *Dermochelys coriacea* (the largest sea turtle, reaching about 8 feet in length), found from CA to WA mainly in Jun–Oct (the animals here nest on beaches in Indonesia!). Leatherback lacks a hard shell, and its back has 5 distinct ridges, but often all you see is a head projecting above the water, and then the animal dives. The other sea turtle species have hard shells, but identifying them to species at sea can be difficult.

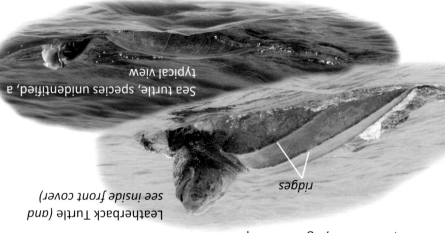

Leatherback Turtle (and
see inside front cover)

ridges

Sea turtle, species unidentified, a
typical view

Jellyfish. On some trips you may see 100s, even 1000s of jellyfish, but on most trips none are seen. Often they are commonest inshore, in slightly murky water, and numerous species occur off the West Coast. Among the most frequently seen are the large, brownish-orange sea nettles (genus *Chrysaora*), the well-named egg-yolk (or fried egg) jellyfish *Phacellophora camtschatica*, and the medium-size, ghostly moon jellies (genus *Aurelia*).

Moon jelly

Egg-yolk jelly

Sea nettles

tentacles extended

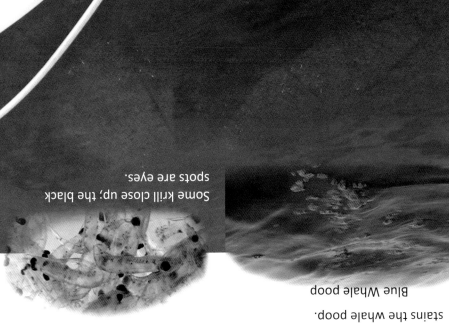

Some krill close up; the black
spots are eyes.

Blue Whale poop

Krill. Small crustaceans, like tiny shrimp. There are numerous species around the world, mainly in colder waters; the two main West Coast species are *Euphausia pacifica* and *Thysanoessa spinifera.* You may see them as swirling pink 'stains' in the water (below), and individuals can even be seen as tiny pink streaks, about an inch long. Krill are a vital part of the food web and are consumed by many creatures, from giant Blue Whales to tiny Cassin's Auklets—seeing these 2 species feeding together is a good clue that krill are present. The pink pigment even from krill stains the whale poop.

By-the-wind Sailor (Velella) *Velella velella.* Some years, mainly in spring—summer, countless 1000s of this free-floating hydrozoan (a jellyfish cousin) can be blown into bands on the sea surface and often wash ashore on beaches. Each Velella measures 2–4 inches across, with a blue mantle and a stiff silvery sail—its only means of locomotion.

Seaweed (also known as algae) often breaks off and drifts out to sea, offering places for birds to rest. The largest seaweeds in the world are **Giant Kelp** *Macrocystis pyrifera* (s. Alaska to Mexico), and **Bull Kelp** *Nereocystis luetkeana* (Alaska to cen. California). Both grow in underwater forests along the coast, where strands can be over 100 feet long and grow more than a foot in a day! Beware: float bladders and mats of Bull Kelp sometimes look like marine mammals resting at the surface.

Buller's Shearwater resting on Bull Kelp.

Landbirds. But wait, isn't this book about *offshore* wildlife? Sure enough, but every spring and fall millions of landbirds migrate, and many of them fly over water, some intentionally, others not. Especially in fall, when inexperienced young are migrating, you may see the occasional landbird far out at sea, ranging from owls and doves to warblers and sparrows. Exhausted birds often land on boats and sometimes even on people!

This wayward Blackpoll Warbler Setophaga striata rested on a whale researcher near Cordell Bank.

Brown-headed Cowbird Molothrus ater is one of the songbirds most frequently seen offshore, here experiencing a marine toilet!

Species Codes, Scientific Names, and Index

Mammals

Birds

Species Codes, Scientific Names, and Index (cont.)

The West Coast (opposite). Dark blue dots show selected ports from which pelagic trips originate. To find out about trips, simply Google, for example, 'California whale watching trips', or 'Oregon seabird pelagic trips' and this should lead you to a list of operators, trips, and dates.